I

The Owl and the Pussy-cat went to sea
  In a beautiful pea-green boat,
They took some honey, and plenty of money,
  Wrapped up in a five-pound note.
The Owl looked up to the stars above,
  And sang to a small guitar,
"O lovely Pussy! O Pussy, my love,
  What a beautiful Pussy you are,
    You are,
    You are!
What a beautiful Pussy you are!"

II

Pussy said to the Owl, "You elegant fowl!
  How charmingly sweet you sing!
O let us be married! too long we have tarried:
  But what shall we do for a ring?"
They sailed away, for a year and a day,
  To the land where the Bong-Tree grows
And there in a wood a Piggy-wig stood
  With a ring at the end of his nose,
    His nose,
    His nose,
With a ring at the end of his nose.

III

"Dear Pig, are you willing to sell for one shilling
  Your ring?" Said the Piggy, "I will."
So they took it away, and were married next day
  By the Turkey who lives on the hill.
They dined on mince, and slices of quince,
  Which they ate with a runcible spoon;
And hand in hand, on the edge of the sand,
  They danced by the light of the moon,
    The moon,
    The moon,
They danced by the light of the moon.

—Edward Lear

THE BOY WHO BECAME A PARROT

A FOOLISH BIOGRAPHY OF EDWARD LEAR, WHO INVENTED NONSENSE

written by
Wolverton Hill

illustrated by
Laura Carlin

Enchanted Lion Books
NEW YORK

WHO was EdWArD LEaR?

Edward Lear was a wildly imaginative man best known for his humorous short verse and "The Owl and the Pussy-cat"—Britain's most beloved children's poem. He was also a brilliant painter who saw beauty in people and places ignored by others. He loved animals, music, travel, chocolate shrimps, pancakes, and his cat, Foss. And unlike most grownups, he preferred children who sometimes misbehave.

"How pleasant to know Mr. Lear!" someone said.

But don't take their word for it.
See for yourself!

In 1812, a boy named Edward
was born into a house full of children,
the 20th child of Jeremiah and Ann Lear.

He was also born into a place full of strange and wondrous animals—London, England, where every Sunday an elephant named Chunee took a stroll through the city past the Exeter Exchange, a building where circus animals, including roaring lions and tigers, were kept on the second floor.

When Edward was just four years old, his parents fell on hard times and sent him to live with his older sisters. Educated at home, he learned to paint and draw, and he devoured books devoted to plants and animals, mythology and adventure. From this early age, he began to dream of faraway places, both real and imagined.

Edward's sisters doted on him and his days were largely happy. But there were dark days, too. Edward suffered from a brain disorder called epilepsy, which caused him to have seizures. Embarrassed by these attacks, he would hide himself away whenever he felt a seizure coming on. He called epilepsy his Demon and it shadowed him for the rest of his life.

The only person who ever knew Edward's secret
was his oldest sister, Ann,
who became like a mother to him.
They shared a love of nature, wordplay,
and stories that made them laugh.
To entertain the two of them,
Edward began writing his own silly stories
and poems, and inventing new words.

Edward also continued to paint and draw, copying detailed illustrations of exotic plants and animals from popular magazines. Before long, he was quite good. So good, in fact, that he was able to sell his drawings on street corners to buy bread and cheese. People began to take notice of his talent. Important people.

And then, in 1828, when Edward was still a teenager, London Zoo opened.

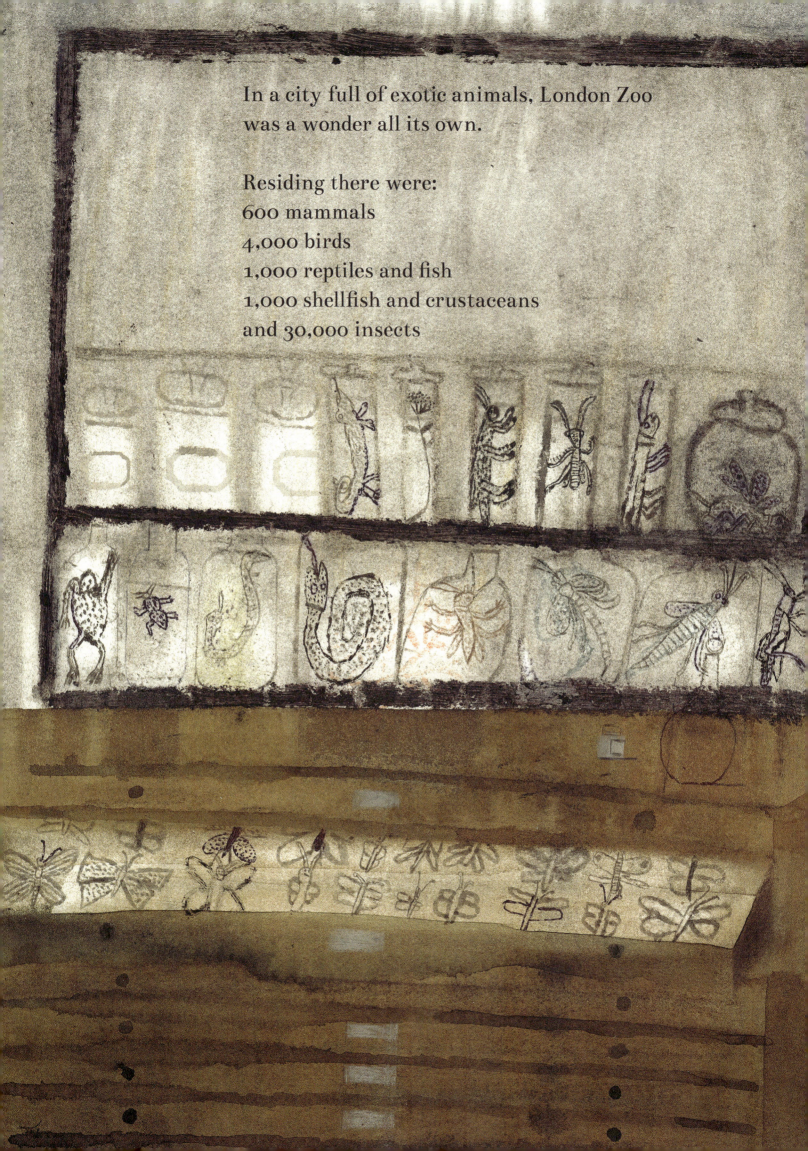

In a city full of exotic animals, London Zoo was a wonder all its own.

Residing there were:
600 mammals
4,000 birds
1,000 reptiles and fish
1,000 shellfish and crustaceans
and 30,000 insects

This wasn't a zoo as we know them today. This was a scientific zoo, for the study of animals. Members only. And one of those members had recognized Edward's talent in the drawings he hawked on the street, and hired him to draw the zoo's residents.

Suddenly, Edward found himself in the company of the most important scientists in the Western world. Even more exciting, he found himself in the company of some of the most remarkable creatures he had ever seen.

He met an otter and a lynx.
An emu and a zebra.
A seal and a flamingo.
An Arabian oryx, a greater kudu, a quagga, and a thylacine.
An orangutan, a wombat, a Tasmanian devil, and a long-nosed potoroo.
Llamas, monkeys, bears.
Three one-hump camels and one hippopotamus.
And parrots. Lots of parrots.

These brilliant birds were one of the zoo's biggest attractions. Members and guests flocked to their cages to gawk at them.

One day, Edward was drawing a blue-and-yellow macaw when a man walked up and stared at the bird. Then he stared at Edward, who was sitting in the cage. It was as if the man couldn't decide which was the more curious specimen—bird or boy.

When the man walked away, the macaw turned to Edward and said, "Have you finished me?"

A stunned Edward watched the macaw jump towards him and grab his sketchbook. Edward had drawn the bird staring back at the man.

"Quite good! Quite good!" said the macaw, his head bobbing rapidly up and down.

Edward smiled. He watched with astonishment as the macaw began to turn the pages, using its thick, black tongue like a thumb.

"That's a rock hyrax," Edward explained.
"And that's a chimpanzee. And that's a kangaroo."
Edward relished saying these strange names out loud.

"Where do these creatures live?" asked the macaw.

"Well they *come* from all over the world," said Edward. "But they live in England now. Here at the zoo, or on private estates. I'm helping to make a visual record of these collections."

"Collections!" scoffed the macaw. "So I'm nothing more than part of a collection?"

The remark stung. Edward took great pride in his skill as an artist and his privileged place at the zoo. But he understood why the bird was upset. New animals were being brought in from all over the world, all the time. People wanted to see them and learn about them—but also to own them. And Edward was helping to catalog these specimens.

Edward felt a kinship with the animals.
In a way, he had been taken from his home, too.
And this sympathy showed in his work.

As one admirer put it, Lear's watercolors "displayed a feeling for the fast beat of a heart, the wetness of a twitching nose, the stress of animals far from their familiar habitat."

By the age of 20, Edward Lear was regarded as one of England's foremost natural history artists. He was also witty and charming, and was invited everywhere.

But he never felt like he truly belonged, ashamed as he was of his humble background—and his Demon.

One day, Edward showed the macaw a new drawing of a big blue bird, wings outstretched and its long, spiked tail extended, streaking across a tropical sky. The bird's eyes were focused on something outside of the frame—on some faraway place he was determined to reach.

"I often think about what it must feel like to soar," said Edward.

The macaw lifted his head,
as if recalling a distant memory.
"There's nothing like it."

Edward drew himself as
a bird throughout his life.
He liked to imagine being
in flight and completely free.

Eventually, thanks to his great talent, Edward was asked by the zoo's president, the Earl of Derby, to draw his impressive private collection of animals. And so it was that Edward began traveling to a place called Knowsley Hall, the Earl's country estate.

Knowsley was no ordinary estate. In the park surrounding his home, the earl kept more than 1,000 live birds and almost 400 live mammals, including a roaming mob of kangaroos! But for Edward, the children were the most engaging and curious species of all.

These were a jumble-bumble of England's finest—the sons and daughters of British nobility who gathered at the estate. Their parents were Very Important People who believed that for everything that could be done, there was a proper way of doing it. Naturally, children don't tend to like rules nearly as much as grownups do, and in Edward, they quickly sensed an ally.

For one, he was an artist, and he entered the house through the back door and ate downstairs with the staff. What's more, he seemed to enjoy their company!

When, to his surprise, Lord Derby began to notice all the children fleeing the dinner table as soon as they were allowed, he asked, "Why?" and "What *is* it?"

His grandson explained: "It's so much more amusing downstairs because that fellow drawing the birds for you is such good company. We so like to hear him talk!"

The children had drawn Edward out of his shell and revealed what would prove to be his most enduring gift—the ability to make people laugh.

Soon, Lord Derby began inviting Edward upstairs to entertain the adults with amusing stories and songs. But for Edward, his new station among what he called "lofty society" was a bore. He wrote to friends, "There is nothing I long for half so much as to giggle and hop on one leg through the house."

With the children,
Edward could be mischievous.

"Boys and girls," he said one day,
"have your parents told you
where children *really* come from?"
And he turned his sketchbook around to show
them a drawing of a remarkable plant,
labeled *Manypeeplia Upsidownia*.

The children gasped.

"*Manypeeplia* grows on the Humbly Islands, where the Scroobious Pip lives," said Edward, showing them the Pip.

The children couldn't make heads or tails (or legs or wings) of it.

"Impossible!" a girl named Violet insisted. "I would have heard of the Scroobious Pip, or *Manypeeplia Upsidownia,* or *Cockatoo Superba,*" she added, showing the others a picture of an iris-like plant abloom with a splendid white parrot.

"Impossible? Wouldn't some people say the same about the African crown crane?" asked Edward, pointing to a long-legged bird that looked hilariously overdressed. "Have you ever seen such an unusual bird?"

Violet folded her arms across her chest. "Of course, silly. I see that bird every day."

That was one of Edward's favorite things about children—the odd and the unusual didn't seem to faze them at all.

He never wanted them to outgrow this, and he encouraged this sense of acceptance in the stories he invented for them.

"Children, do you know how Knowsley Hall got its name?"

Fitzwilliam explained that he had recently met a fellow called a Pobble... who had to wrap his nose in red flannel, lest his toes fall off.

The Pobble was in need of more flannel, which could only be had by crossing the Cornish Channel.

But the swift channel currents swept the flannel right off his nose!

And a porpoise carried off all his toes!

Dear Fitzwilliam! Let me give you an estate. And a carriage speckled with gold driven by a coachman in green vestments and silver spectacles, with lofty cushions made of muffins. And Pobbles can live here, too, and make new toes from tree nuts!

"What happened to all these nosy people?" asked Violet.

"Why," said Edward, with a wink, "just look around! Is it not still a world of interesting noses?"

The children's eyes darted around while they self-consciously touched their own noses.

"By welcoming all these remarkable people to Knowsley Hall, the first Earl of Derby created a place where the common and the uncommon could live side by side, so that even a bird like the crowned crane seems perfectly ordinary."

Violet and the other children nodded, happy that their little corner of the world included many unusual birds and animals, and now, the very unusual grownup named Edward Lear.

THERE WAS AN OLD MAN OF WHITEHAVEN,
WHO DANCED A QUADRILLE WITH A RAVEN;
BUT THEY SAID—'IT'S ABSURD, TO ENCOURAGE THIS BIRD!'
SO THEY SMASHED THAT OLD MAN OF WHITEHAVEN.

THERE WAS AN OLD PERSON OF EWELL,
WHO CHIEFLY SUBSISTED ON GRUEL;
BUT TO MAKE IT MORE NICE, HE INSERTED SOME MICE,
WHICH REFRESHED THAT OLD A PERSON OF EWELL.

In all, Edward visited Knowsley Hall from 1831 to 1837, to make paintings of Lord Derby's birds and mammals. While there, he began writing *limericks*—short, song-like poems with shocks of suspense and humor. The children loved Edward's limericks because it felt like he was breaking rules, using the traditional form of poetry to say things no adult would ever say. For once, a grownup was on their side.

THERE WAS AN OLD MAN WITH A BEARD
Who Said, 'IT IS JUST AS I FEARED!—
TWO OWLS AND A HEN,
FOUR LARKS
AND A WREN,
HAVE ALL BUILT THEIR NESTS IN MY BEARD!'

THERE WAS AN OLD MAN WITH A NOSE,
WHO SAID, 'IF You Choose To Suppose,
THAT MY NOSE IS TOO LONG, YOU ARE CERTAINLY WRONG!'
THAT REMARKABLE Man WITH a NOSE.

Edward and the children conspired to create an outrageous universe where people lived in jars, on walls, in wheelbarrows, and perched in trees. They travelled atop crocodiles, tortoises, hares, and bears. Their absurdly large beards were home to other critters, and hats became houses. Ducks were best friends with kangaroos, and men danced with birds.

In 1846 Lear published *A Book of Nonsense,* illustrated by himself—a collection of many of the limericks he had first shared with the children at Knowsley Hall. The book proved to be as popular with adults as it was with children. Nonsense offered a fabulous refuge from a real world that too often made no sense.

Such temporary escapes from reality became more and more important to Edward as he grew older. He felt smothered by the constraints of English society, and he longed for a place where he could really feel at home. And so after Knowsley, he embarked on a new adventure that would last the rest of his life: traveling the world and inventing his own.

Edward left England in 1837. That summer, he met an American family whose youngest child, Daisy, found the hotel dining room frightful, surrounded as she was by strange people eating strange food with too many different kinds of forks, knives, and spoons.

One day, Edward pushed a drawing across the table to her. It was a very scientific-looking drawing of a Fork Tree. Daisy laughed, and before long, she and "Uncle Lear" were the best of friends.

As a world traveler, Edward turned his painting skills to landscapes. But while other artists flocked to tourist spots, Edward traveled to remote places, often at great risk. Once, he was captured by bandits. Another time, he was chased by a wild bull.

He was awarded many commissions, and even gave young Queen Victoria drawing lessons. This gave him the means to build a home, which he did in Italy, where he felt more free.

The one thing now missing from his life was true companionship.

He often thought of marrying, but to Edward, traditional marriage seemed like ill-fitting shoes: "Far too tight!"

Indeed, some of his most famous poems— "The Duck and the Kangaroo" and "The Owl and the Pussy-cat"—are about unconventional unions. But he understood that such odd couplings could only happen in the world of nonsense.

Edward did, at last, find himself a companion: a cat named Foss, whose tail had been cut to a stump.

They spent the next
16 years together.

Edward loved drawing himself and Foss together in his poems and in letters to friends, and Foss became quite famous in his own right.

When Foss died in July of 1887, Edward's grief was profound. He buried his beloved friend beneath a fig tree in his garden.

Just six months later, Edward passed away, too.

His gravestone in San Remo reads, "A Landscape Painter in Many Lands," an appreciation of his sensitive renderings of the natural world.

But the words also speak to the power of his imagination to conjure entirely new lands, with their own joyfully strange people, plants, and animals. Worlds full of wonder, inviting to us all.

Some of Edward Lear's works

Lear was hired by leading ornithologists to provide illustrations for their books, such as this Eagle Owl for John Gould's *The Birds of Europe*.

The now-extinct Great Auk, another of Lear's illustrations for Gould's *The Birds of Europe*, was actually credited to Gould himself. This was probably an accident, but if you look closely at the bottom right of this print and of the Eagle Owl, you'll see that Lear embedded his own name in each of his pieces.

TESTUDO PARDALIS, Bell.

For his book devoted to turtles, including this Leopard Tortoise, Thomas Bell used Lear's skill as a lithographer to make the prints, while another artist hand-colored them. Lithography was a relatively new printing technique, and Lear took great pains to master it. Though he would call lithography "the old enemy," he became so skilled at it that the Royal Society of Arts later sought his professional advice.

"A huge Macaw is now looking me in the face as much as to say — 'finish me'," Lear wrote to a friend. His book of parrots, titled *Illustrations of the Family of Psittacidae, or Parrots,* appeared in fourteen volumes between 1830 and 1832 and was the first of its kind to focus on a single species.

Years after Lear had left Knowsley Hall, Lord Derby published seventeen of his favorite Lear illustrations in a book titled *Gleanings from the Menagerie and Aviary at Knowsley Hall*, including this Red Macauco, or Red Lemur.

Lear's own illustration for "The Owl and the Pussy-cat," from 1871, was commemorated on a stamp by Britain's Royal Mail in 1988.

A Note on the Art

Sharp-eyed readers will have noticed that on pages 30-31, they were browsing past a gallery of Edward Lear's own natural history illustrations.

But you might not have noticed a few of Lear's nonsense drawings popping up in other places, too,

like here,

and here,

and here,

right in the middle of dinner!

Laura Carlin's Scroobious Pip isn't the only one in the book. If you turn the page, you'll find, below the Author's Note, Lear's own drawing of the Scroobious Pip. He doodled it at the bottom of a poem about the Pip that he was writing at the time of his death.

Author's Note

When Edward was working on his parrot illustrations, he wrote to a friend that "for the last 12 months I have so moved—thought—looked at,—& existed among Parrots—that should any transmigration take place at my decease I am sure my soul would be very uncomfortable in anything but one of the Psittacidae."

One of those illustrations, labeled "hyacinth macaw," turned out to be an entirely new species. The French ornithologist, Charles Lucien Bonaparte, nephew of Napoleon, named it Lear's Macaw. So Edward did, in a way, become a parrot.

Lear has long been a hero of mine. I love wordplay and silly puns and foolishness in general, so to discover that an actual, famous, grownup writer had made nonsense respectable was inspiring. The influence of Lear is all over my first book for children, which starred a puffin—a funny little bird that looks like something a nonsense writer would invent.

I always wondered why Lear wasn't as well-known as Alice's creator, Lewis Carroll. Then I discovered that my nonsense hero had been, for a brief time, a natural history artist so talented that he was admired by John J. Audubon. And later he had become a landscape painter and travel writer hired by Queen Victoria to give her drawing lessons. It turns out I didn't know much about him either!

It's hard to find a children's book author who was a greater ally of children. Kids loved Edward Lear. He understood how absurd it could feel to navigate the complicated world of grownups in little more than a pea-green boat. He really was on their side.

I can't put it better than the poet W.H. Auden, one of the many artists and writers who were influenced by or admired Lear. "Children swarmed to him like settlers," he wrote. "He became a land."

—*Wolverton Hill*

Lear Timeline

1812: Edward Lear is born on May 12th at Bowman's Lodge, Highgate, London.

1816: Sent away by his mother to live with his eldest sister, Ann, after his father loses the family fortune on the Stock Exchange. Edward will never get over this.

1817: Begins having epileptic seizures, which he calls his "Demon."

1825: Writes his oldest surviving poem, "Eclogue."

1827: Moves with Ann to a flat at 38 Upper North Place, Gray's Inn Road.

1827: Begins selling drawings (mainly medical drawings for hospitals and doctors) to buy bread and cheese.

1828: The Zoological Society of London opens.

1830: Begins drawing parrots at London Zoo and issues the first two folios of *Illustrations of the Family of Psitticidae, or Parrots*.

1831: Invited to Knowsley Hall, home of Lord Stanley, 13th Earl of Derby, to begin drawing his personal collection of animals. Lord Stanley owns a book called *Anecdotes and Adventures of Fifteen Gentlemen*, which introduces Edward to the limerick. Edward begins writing nonsense in secret.

1832: Moves out on his own for the first time, to 61 Albany Street in Regent's Park, near the Zoo.

1833: Edward's father dies.

1835: Inspired by visits abroad, Edward begins painting landscapes.

1837: Poor eyesight causes him to abandon natural history illustration. He moves to Italy and will spend the rest of his life traveling and painting landscapes.

1841: Publishes his first travel book, *Views in Rome and Its Environs*.

1846: Tutors Queen Victoria on the Isle of Wight after she admires his painting.

1846: Publishes *A Book of Nonsense* under the name "old Derry down Derry"; Lord Derby publishes *Gleanings from the Menagerie and Aviary at Knowsley Hall* featuring Lear's illustrations from a decade earlier.

1851: Meets Alfred Tennyson, Britain's poet laureate, and his wife Emily. Plans to begin illustrating Tennyson's poems.

1855: Edward's art exhibited at the prestigious Royal Society of British Artists for the first time.

1861: His sister, Ann, dies. Edward is devastated.

1861: Publishes a third edition of of *A Book of Nonsense*, this time under his own name.

1865: Lewis Carroll publishes *Alice's Adventures in Wonderland*, likely inspired by Lear's nonsense writing.

1870: Publishes "The Owl and the Pussy-cat" in *Nonsense Songs, Stories, Botany, and Alphabets*. It will become Britain's most beloved children's poem.

1871: Moves to San Remo, Italy, into Villa Emily, named after Emily Tennyson.

1872: His beloved cat, Foss, arrives.

1876: Publishes "The Dong with a Luminous Nose" and "The Courtship of Yonghy-Bonghy-Bo," two poems about lost love, in *Laughable Lyrics*.

1887: Foss dies and is buried by Edward in his garden, with a headstone that reads, "Below is buried my good cat Foss."

1888: Edward dies on January 29th, while illustrating poems by Alfred Tennyson. He is buried in San Remo.

To Charlie, my very own Foss — W. H.

To Tom and Edward — L. C.

Many thanks to Derek Johns of The Edward Lear Society and Marco Graziosi, creator of A Blog of Bosh, for reading early drafts and offering advice and encouragement. Also thanks to the Academy of Natural Sciences of Drexel University, Library and Archives and Houghton Library, Harvard University for providing images of Lear's artwork. – Wolverton Hill

Lear's images in order of appearance:
Eagle Owl, Academy of Natural Sciences of Drexel University, Library and Archives (QL690 A1G6) | *Great Auk*, Academy of Natural Sciences of Drexel University, Library and Archives (QL690 A1G6) | *Leopard Tortoise*, Academy of Natural Sciences of Drexel University, Library and Archives (QL666 C5B4) | *Blue and Yellow Macaw*, Houghton Library, Harvard University (Typ 805L.32 (A) plate 8) | *Red Macauco*, Academy of Natural Sciences of Drexel University, Library and Archives (QL73D 4D3) | *The Owl and the Pussy-cat*, Houghton Library, Harvard University (MS Typ 55.14 (105)) | *Kangaroo*, Houghton Library, Harvard University (MS Typ 55.12 (fol. 17)) | *Chimpanzee*, Houghton Library, Harvard University (MS Typ 55.12) | *Rock Hyrax*, Houghton Library, Harvard University (MS Typ 55.12 (fol. 4)) | *Manypeeplia Upsidownia*, Houghton Library, Harvard University (MS Typ 55.13 (13)) | *Cockatooka Superba*, Houghton Library, Harvard University (MS Eng 797.1 (fol. 1)) | *Fork Tree*, Houghton Library, Harvard University (55.14, item 33) | *Scroobius Pip*, Houghton Library, Harvard University (MS Typ 55.14, Box 2:159)

www.enchantedlion.com

First edition published in 2025 by Enchanted Lion Books,
248 Creamer Street, Studio 4, Brooklyn, NY 11231
Text copyright © 2025 by Barry Wolverton
Illustrations copyright © 2025 by Laura Carlin
Book design by Dasha Tolstikova
All rights reserved under International and Pan-American Copyright Conventions
A CIP record is on file with the Library of Congress

ISBN 978-1-59270-413-2

Printed in Italy by Società Editoriale Grafiche AZ, S.r.l
Distributed throughout the world by ABRAMS, New York

First Printing